LIFE
ON EARTH

THE STORY OF EVOLUTION

WITHDRAW

BY STEVE JENKINS

HOUGHTON MIFFLIN BOSTON 2002

Rabbits, cacti, bumblebees, jellyfish, penguins, sunflowers—all living things on the earth are the descendants of simple, single-celled organisms that lived more than 3½ billion years ago.

Millions and millions. There are millions of different kinds of plants and animals living on the earth. Many millions more lived here in the past. Where did they all come from? Why have some died out and others lived on?

In the beginning. The earth is more than 4½ billion years old. For a long time, life couldn't exist here. The ground was hot enough to melt rocks. There was no liquid water. Comets and asteroids frequently crashed into the surface, and volcanoes erupted constantly, filling the air with poisonous gases.

The first life. Living things differ from those that aren't alive in several ways. Something that is alive uses energy, gets rid of wastes, responds to its environment, and makes more of itself by reproducing. Because conditions on the early earth were so harsh, it took a long time for the first life to develop. By the time the earth was a few hundred million years old, its surface had cooled enough for water to collect and form oceans. By 3½ billion years ago, microscopic bacteria were thriving in these oceans.

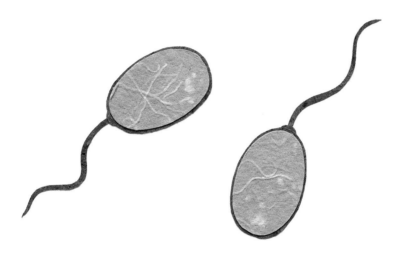

No one knows when or where life began. Perhaps it formed in a warm, shallow sea or a mud puddle. It might have developed first in sea spray, deep in the ocean, or underground. Life might even have arrived on the earth inside an asteroid.

A brief history of life. For more than a billion years, primitive bacteria were the only form of life on the earth. As time went by, new living things appeared, at first in the seas and later on land. Eventually, life could be found almost everywhere on the planet.

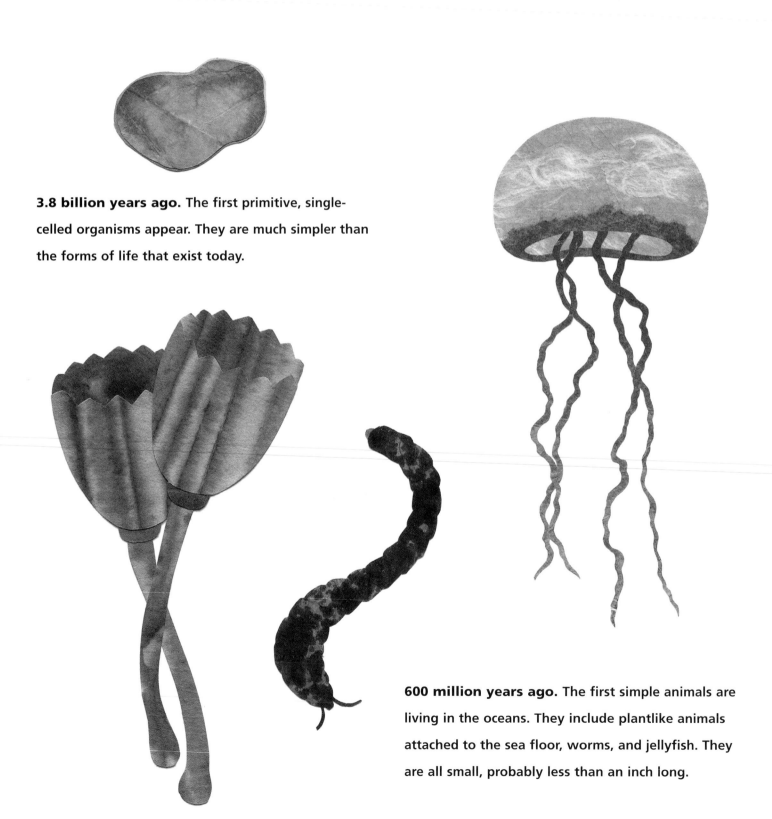

3.8 billion years ago. The first primitive, single-celled organisms appear. They are much simpler than the forms of life that exist today.

600 million years ago. The first simple animals are living in the oceans. They include plantlike animals attached to the sea floor, worms, and jellyfish. They are all small, probably less than an inch long.

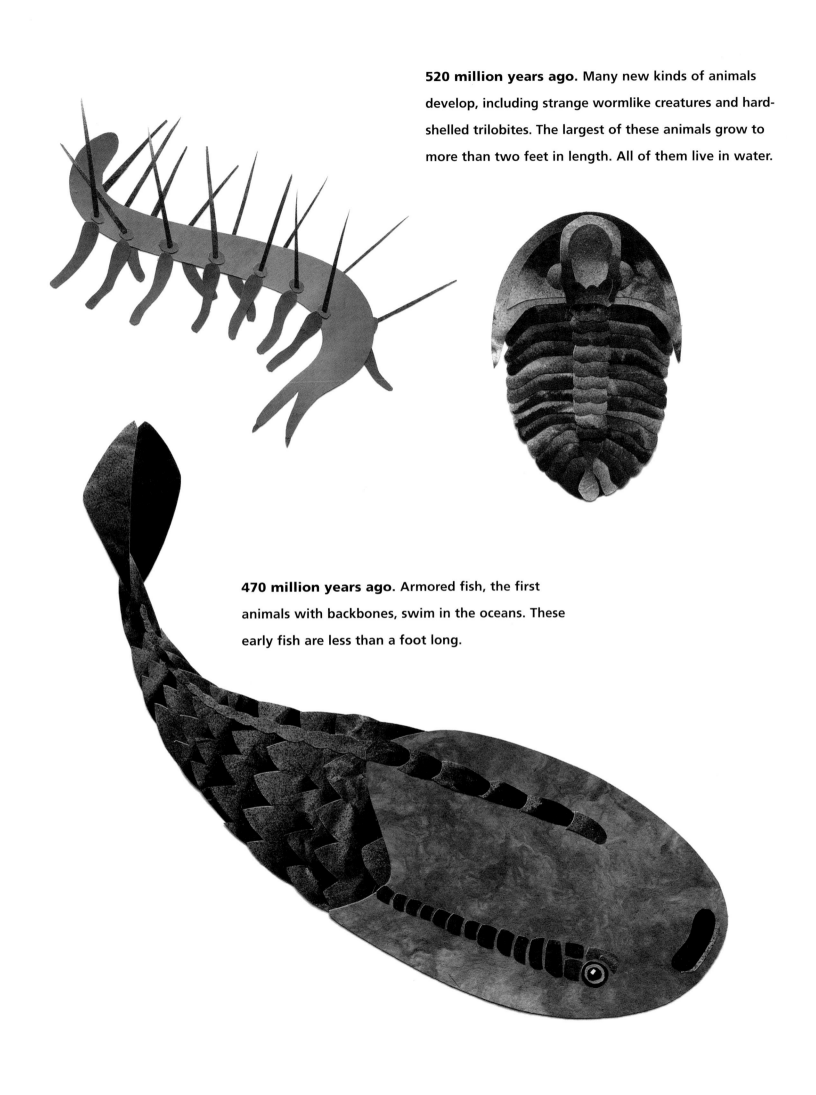

520 million years ago. Many new kinds of animals develop, including strange wormlike creatures and hard-shelled trilobites. The largest of these animals grow to more than two feet in length. All of them live in water.

470 million years ago. Armored fish, the first animals with backbones, swim in the oceans. These early fish are less than a foot long.

420 million years ago. Shellfish, nautiluses, and corals swim in the water or live on the ocean floor.

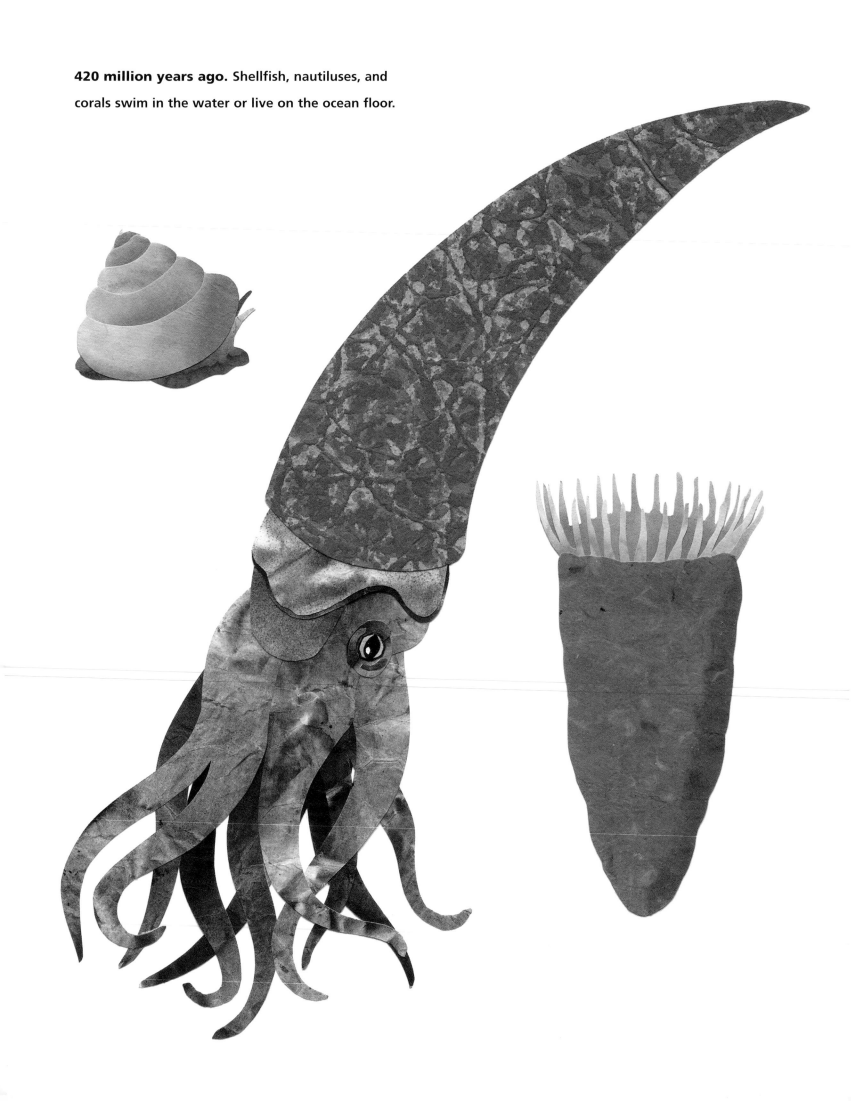

400 million years ago. Mosses and ferns move from the water onto the land, followed by centipedes, insects, and the first amphibians. The first plants and animals to live on land are quite small.

330 million years ago. Giant ferns and club mosses form huge swampy forests, and insects become the first flying animals. Dragonflies with wings two feet across fly among plants that grow to heights of fifty feet or more.

290 million years ago. The age of reptiles begins. The first reptiles are small animals, about a foot long, and look much like today's lizards.

230 million years ago. One or more groups of reptiles evolve into dinosaurs. They range from bird-like animals a few inches tall to giants more than 90 feet long. They live in the sea, on the land, and in the air. Dinosaurs will be the dominant animals on the earth for the next 160 million years.

215 million years ago. A different group of reptiles develops into the first mammals. For the next 150 million years, mammals remain small in size and are active mainly at night. This helps them avoid being eaten by dinosaurs.

150 million years ago. The first birds, probably relatives of tree-climbing dinosaurs, take to the air.

65 million years ago. The last of the dinosaurs become extinct, and large flightless birds, some more than seven feet tall, become the dominant meat eaters on land. Flowering plants appear.

40 million years ago. With the dinosaurs gone, mammals are able to evolve into large plant eaters and predators. This rhinolike animal, called "battering ram beast," is nearly as big as an elephant.

5 million years ago. The ancestors of early humans, descended from apes, are living in Africa. They are the first apelike animals to walk upright.

130,000 years ago. Modern humans—people who look like us—appear in the Middle East and Africa.

As life forms develop, many plants and animals become larger and more complex. But they do not replace the smaller, simpler forms of life. Today, after 3½ billion years, bacteria—some of the first living things on the earth—are still evolving and are among the most numerous and successful forms of life.

Why have so many different forms of life developed on the earth? People wondered about this for a long time. About 150 years ago, an Englishman named Charles Darwin proposed a theory to explain how and why new forms of life develop. His explanation, called the theory of evolution, is one of the great accomplishments of science.

A new world. A few hundred years ago, most people believed that all plants and animals were created at the same time, in the not-too-

distant past. They believed that living things hadn't changed, that they had been the same since their creation. New discoveries, however, were beginning to alter the way many people thought.

Explorers were returning from distant places with forms of life that most people had never seen before. As scientists studied these plants and animals, they saw that many of them were like those they already knew. Meanwhile, scientists were creating systems to organize living things by placing them into groups. They called a group of plants or animals that had similar features and that could produce offspring a *species*.

Perhaps, the scientists thought, many different plants and animals had come from the same ancestors and had changed over time. Scientists were also finding that the earth was much older than anyone had imagined. It looked as if life had had a long time to develop.

In various parts of the world, new fossils—the preserved remains of ancient life—were being unearthed. Many of these fossils were clearly the bones of animals that no longer existed. Once more, it seemed likely that life had not always remained the same.

These ideas and discoveries were making it clear that all living things had come from earlier forms of life, many of which no longer existed.

The theory of evolution. In 1831 a ship named the *Beagle* left England to sail around the world on a scientific expedition. The scientist and naturalist Charles Darwin was aboard. Over the next five years, he observed and collected plants and animals from many parts of the world. After he returned to England, he spent years studying what he had collected and thinking about the things he had seen. Finally, combining his own ideas with those of earlier scientists, he was able to develop the theory of evolution.

On his voyage, Darwin visited the Galápagos, an isolated group of islands in the Pacific Ocean. There, among other unique forms of life, he found a unusual group of finches. These birds gave Darwin important clues about the way evolution works. He believed that all of the finches were the descendants of the same two birds, but he noticed that on each island the birds' beaks were shaped differently. The finches on each island ate different kinds of food, and Darwin believed that small changes in the birds over many generations had resulted in fourteen different species, each with a beak adapted to a particular diet.

The marine iguana lives only in the Galápagos islands.

This finch has a short, strong beak for cracking hard seeds.

This one has a beak that's shaped to hold a twig, used to pry insects from tree bark.

This bird has a curved beak for eating plants and soft fruit.

This finch uses its long beak to catch insects.

Survival of the fittest. The Galápagos finches helped Darwin understand the role played by the environment in evolution. Most plants and animals produce many more offspring than can survive. Many fish, amphibians, and insects lay hundreds or thousands of eggs. If all of the offspring of even a single pair of these animals survived, they would soon overrun the earth. However, almost all of the young perish before they can grow up and lay eggs themselves. Darwin saw that those less fit for their environment—the slower, weaker, and less hardy ones—are more likely to die or be killed. Those best able to escape predators, find food, and survive hardships are the most likely to survive and become parents themselves. Darwin called this process *natural selection*, or *survival of the fittest*.

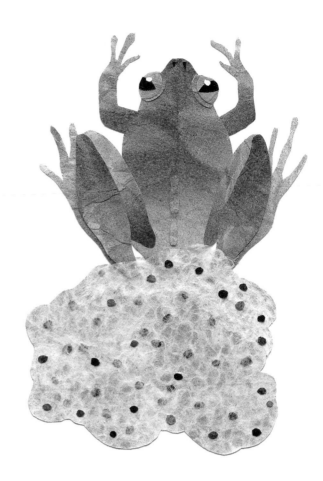

Natural selection at work. A mother frog lays 3,000 eggs. Most of these eggs are eaten by birds and fish. Of the 200 tadpoles that hatch, few survive. Most are eaten by predators. Ten tadpoles live to turn into frogs.

One frog, able to jump
a little farther than its
brothers and sisters,
escapes from predators
and survives.

One is caught by a fox.

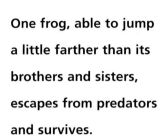

One dies after moving to
a pond that dries up.

Two are eaten by snakes.

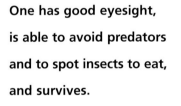

One has good eyesight,
is able to avoid predators
and to spot insects to eat,
and survives.

One can't find enough
insects to eat and starves.

One is eaten by a fish.

One is eaten by a bird.

Of the ten frogs, only two
survive. One is a good
jumper and the other has
sharp eyesight. If they
reproduce, they'll proba-
bly pass on these qualities
to their offspring.

One is eaten by a toad.

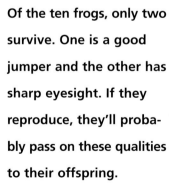

Variation and mutation. It's easy to see that those who are weak or poorly suited to their environment are less likely to survive. What makes some plants and animals more fit—more likely to survive?

Scientists in Darwin's time didn't understand how traits were passed from parents to the next generation. As scientists learned more, they found that offspring could differ from their parents through *variation* or *mutation*.

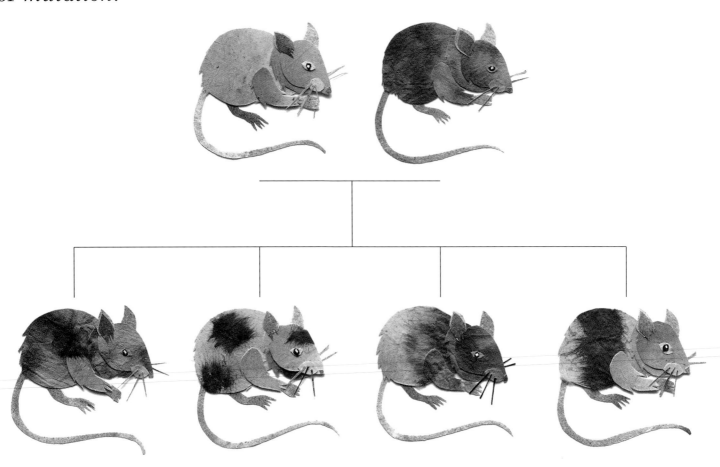

Variation. Many living things reproduce sexually. This means that there is a father and a mother and that each baby has a mixture of the qualities of the parents. Since each mixture is a little different, there are natural differences among offspring. Some will be taller, some shorter; some darker, some lighter; some faster, and some slower. Some of these variations may help the organism survive. A faster mouse, for instance, will be more likely to escape predators and have babies of its own.

Mutation. Sometimes when plants and animals reproduce, something unusual happens and completely new features, called mutations, appear in the next generation. Most mutations are harmful and cause the organism to die. Sometimes, though, they provide an advantage and are passed on.

The parents.

Fish with no mutations. This fish is a lot like its parents.

A helpful mutation. This spotted fish is harder to see on the pebbly bottom of a stream. This fish survives and passes on its spots to some of its children, who are also more likely to survive.

A harmful mutation. This albino fish is completely white. Because a white fish is much easier for a predator to spot, the fish probably does not survive.

New species. The earth is constantly changing. Mountains and rivers form and disappear, oceans rise or dry up, and forests and deserts come and go. Even the continents are moving, and what is a tropical jungle today may be covered with snow and ice in a few million years. These changes, both fast and slow, cause some plants and animals to die out—to become extinct. They also create opportunities for new forms of life to develop.

The first horses lived in dense forests about 55 million years ago. They were only about a foot tall, and their small size let them move easily through the vegetation.

Over millions of years, the earth's climate changed, and many forests were replaced by grasslands. Larger horses with longer legs were better able to escape predators in these open spaces. By 3 million years ago, the modern horse, a completely different species, had evolved.

After many generations, variations and mutations can make a species larger, or more colorful, or different in some other way. Each difference is tested by natural selection: either a change makes a plant or animal better able to survive and pass on new features to its offspring, or it makes survival less likely. After millions of years, accumulated small differences between one generation and the next have become big differences. A new species—a new kind of plant or animal—has been created. This is how evolution works.

Beetles (and more beetles). Some kinds of plants and animals have been very good at evolving new shapes, sizes, and functions to fit changing environments. Beetles, for instance, are found almost everywhere. They live in forests, deserts, water, underground, and even in our houses. There are about 300,000 known species of beetles, and possibly millions more not yet discovered and named.

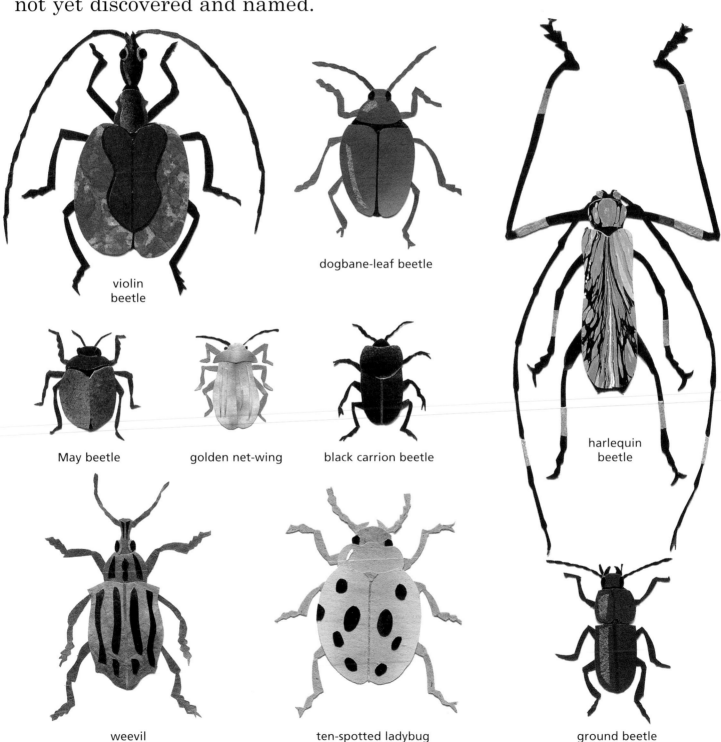

violin
beetle

dogbane-leaf beetle

May beetle

golden net-wing

black carrion beetle

harlequin
beetle

weevil

ten-spotted ladybug

ground beetle

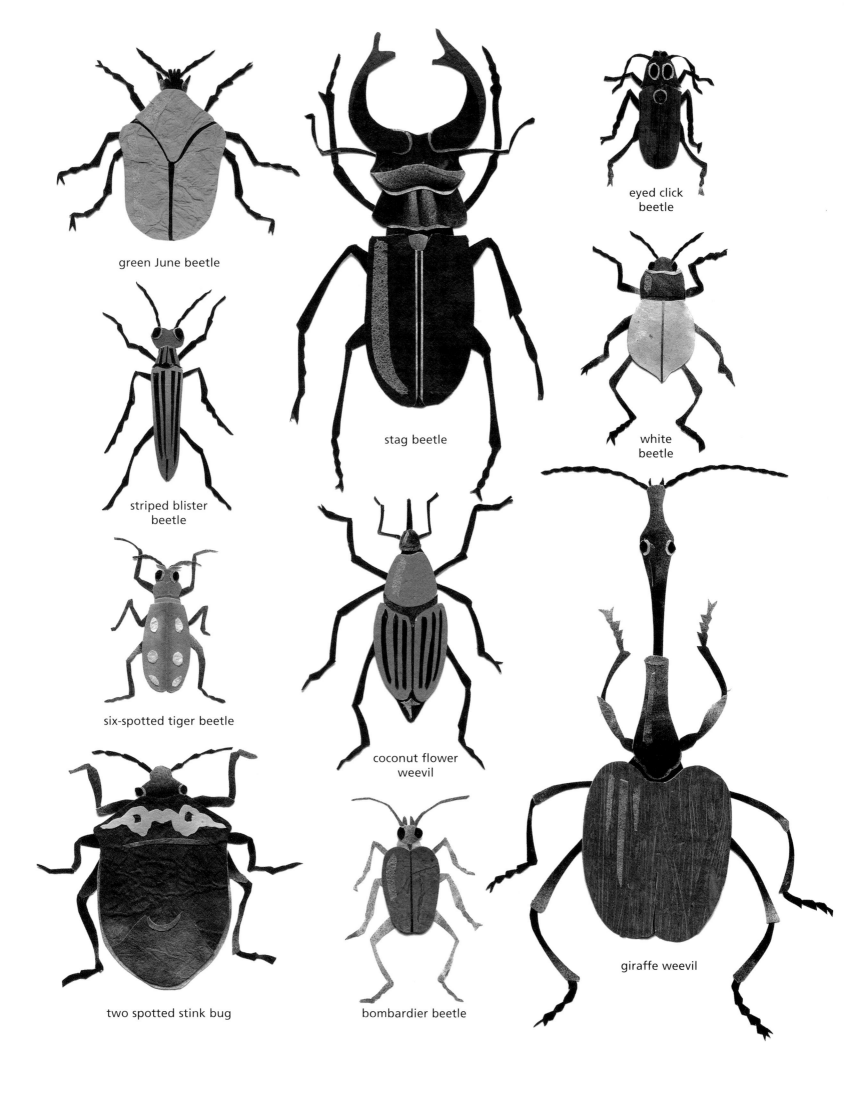

green June beetle

stag beetle

eyed click
beetle

white
beetle

striped blister
beetle

six-spotted tiger beetle

coconut flower
weevil

giraffe weevil

two spotted stink bug

bombardier beetle

Good designs. Some living things have evolved to fit their habitats so well that they haven't changed much in a long time. Here are a few plants and animals with successful, long-lasting designs.

The first **turtles** appeared more than 200 million years ago.

This is a leaf from a **ginkgo tree**. These trees evolved around 220 million years ago, about the same time as the first dinosaurs.

Dragonflies have been here for the past 250 million years.

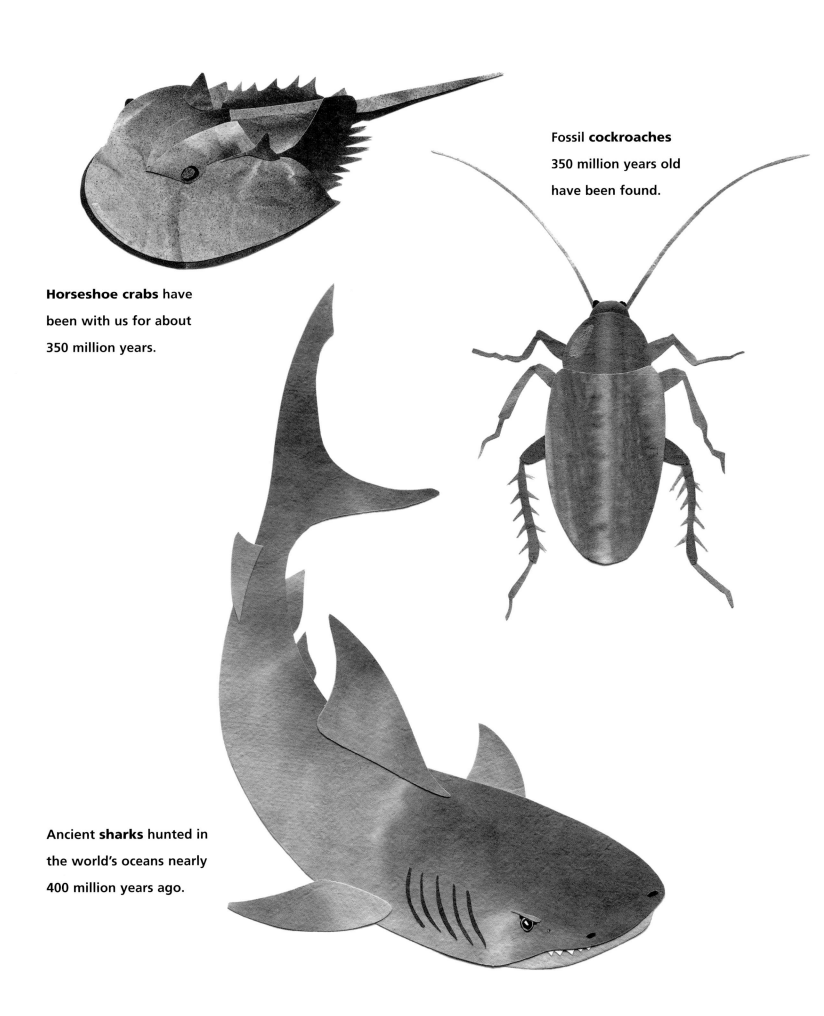

Horseshoe crabs have been with us for about 350 million years.

Fossil **cockroaches** 350 million years old have been found.

Ancient **sharks** hunted in the world's oceans nearly 400 million years ago.

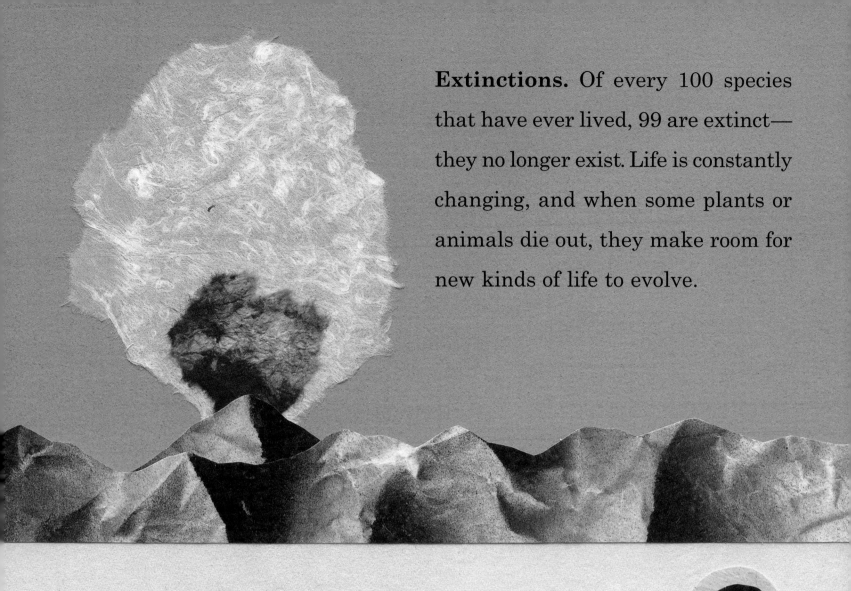

Extinctions. Of every 100 species that have ever lived, 99 are extinct— they no longer exist. Life is constantly changing, and when some plants or animals die out, they make room for new kinds of life to evolve.

Mass extinctions occur when a large number of species die out within a relatively short time. Past mass extinctions—there have been about twenty during the past 1 billion years—were caused by volcanic eruptions, changes in climate, or asteroids crashing into the earth. The extinction that marked the end of the dinosaurs occurred about 65 million years ago and may have been the result of an asteroid hitting the earth. The collision would have thrown up huge clouds of dust and smoke that blocked out the sun and caused most plants to die. Without plants (or plant eaters) for food, many animals couldn't survive.

Dinosaurs disappeared
about 65 million years ago.

Right now the earth is experiencing another mass
extinction. This one is being caused by humans. We
are destroying plants and animals and the places
where they live by building cities and farms and by
polluting the air, soil, and water. Because of human
activity, the earth has lost hundreds of thousands
of species in the last fifty years and may lose half of
all the species alive now in the next hundred years.

The woolly mammoth has
been extinct for about
10,000 years.

The last dodo died in 1681, a
little more than 300 years ago.

A day in the life. It's hard to understand how old the earth really is. The bar below shows our planet's 4½-billion-year history as a single twenty-four-hour day.

(00:00)
The earth forms.

12:00 a.m.	1:00 a.m.	2:00 a.m.	3:00 a.m.	4:00 a.m.	5:00 a.m.	6:00 a.m.	7:00 a.m.	8:00 a.m.	9:00 a.m.	10:00 a.m.	11:00 a.m.	12:00 noon

4:47 a.m.
Life appears.

11:39 p.m.
Dinosaurs become
extinct; flowering
plants appear on
land.

11:59:58 p.m.
(2 seconds before
midnight)
Modern humans
appear.

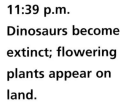

9:52 p.m.
Life moves
to the land.

| 1:00 p.m. | 2:00 p.m. | 3:00 p.m. | 4:00 p.m. | 5:00 p.m. | 6:00 p.m. | 7:00 p.m. | 8:00 p.m. | 9:00 p.m. | 10:00 p.m. | 11:00 p.m. | midnight |

10:42 p.m.
The first dinosaurs
and mammals evolve.

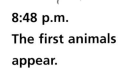

11:58:30 p.m. (1½
minutes before
midnight)
Early humans are
found in Africa.

8:48 p.m.
The first animals
appear.

A key to the animals on pages 4–7. Names of extinct species are in italics.

Millions and millions. There are millions of different kinds of plants and animals living on the earth. Many millions more lived here in the past. Where did they all come from? Why have some died out and others lived on?

1   tiger salamander, North America
2   *club moss, 300 m.y.a. (million years ago)*
3   wallcreeper, Asia
4   ocean trout, worldwide
5   *Macrauchenia, 100,000 years ago*
6   flea, worldwide
7   *Basilosaurus, 40 m.y.a.*
8   peanut worm, oceans worldwide
9   barrel cactus, deserts worldwide
10 green tree frog, United States
11 *northern sea star, 120 m.y.a.*
12 English ivy, worldwide
13 centipede, worldwide
14 opah, warm oceans worldwide
15 amanita, North America
16 vampire bat, South America
17 black rhinoceros, Africa
18 tunicates, sea floors worldwide
19 pink-tailed skink, Mexico
20 lacewing, worldwide
21 whelk tingle, Atlantic Ocean
22 monk seal, Atlantic Ocean and Mediterranean Sea
23 red crab, North America
24 *Hylonomus, 280 m.y.a.*
25 *Megalosaurus, 145 m.y.a.*
26 anenome, oceans worldwide
27 toucan, South America
28 capybara, South America
29 gulper eel, oceans worldwide
30 mangrove leaves, tropics worldwide
31 ameoba, worldwide
32 comb jelly, oceans worldwide
33 strawberry, worldwide
34 black carpenter ant, North America
35 southern carmine bee-eater, Africa
36 *Dolichocebus, 30 m.y.a.*
37 toothed wrack, Atlantic Ocean
38 bear beetle, California
39 ostrich, Africa
40 tube sponge, oceans worldwide
41 hawksbill turtle, oceans worldwide
42 bowhead whale, arctic oceans
43 marbled chiton, Atlantic Ocean
44 plankton, oceans worldwide
45 tarantula, worldwide
46 common mold, worldwide
47 *Thalacines, extinct 1934*

For further reading

Burnie, David, and Don E. Wilson, eds. *Animal.*
London: Dorling Kindersley, 2001.

A large encyclopedia of the animal kingdom
produced with the Smithsonian Institution.
Includes detailed information accompanying
thousands of photos or photo-realistic
illustrations.

Evolution of Life.
Alexandria, Va.: Time-Life, 1992.

An illustrated look at the subject in a question
and answer format. The book asks and answers
specific questions from major periods of life's
development.

Gamlin, Linda. *Eyewitness Books: Evolution.*
London: Dorling Kindersley, 1993.

A visual exploration of the subject.

Garassino, Alessandro. *Life: Origins and Evolution.*
Austin, Tex.: Steck-Vaughn, 1995.

An overview of the origins and development of life,
with many illustrations.

Lindsay, William. *The Great Dinosaur Atlas.*
London: Dorling Kindersley, 1991.

An illustrated, large-format guide to dinosaurs.

Webster, Stephen. *The Kingfisher Book of Evolution.*
New York: Kingfisher, 2000.

An illustrated guide to evolution and the history
of life on earth.

Bibliography

Berra, Tim. *Evolution and the Myth of Creationism.*
Stanford: Stanford University Press, 1990.

Eldredge, Niles. *The Pattern of Evolution.*
New York: W. H. Freeman, 2000.

Eldredge, Niles. *The Triumph of Evolution and
the Failure of Creationism.*
New York: W. H. Freeman, 2000.

Gould, Stephen, ed. *The Book of Life.*
New York: W. W. Norton, 2001.

Jones, Steve. *Darwin's Ghost.*
New York: Random House, 1999.

Osterbrock, Donald, and Peter Raven, eds.
Origins and Extinctions.
Westford, Conn.: Murray Printing Co., 1988.

Weiner, Jonathan. *The Beak of the Finch.*
New York: Knopf, 1994.

For Jamie

www.houghtonmifflinbooks.com

The text is set in Century Schoolbook and Frutiger Bold.
The illustrations are collages of cut and torn paper.

Library of Congress Cataloging-in-Publication Data

Jenkins, Steve, 1952–
Life on earth : the story of evolution / written and illustrated
by Steve Jenkins.
p. cm.
Summary: Provides an overview of the origin and
evolution of life on earth and of what has been learned
from the study of evolution.
ISBN 0-618-16476-6 (hardcover)
1. Evolution (Biology)—Juvenile literature. [1. Evolution
(Biology)] I. Title.
QH367.1 .J46 2002   576.8—dc21   2002000472

Printed in Singapore
TWP 10 9 8 7 6 5 4 3 2 1